How Does the Sky Seem to Change?

HOUGHTON MIFFLIN HARCOURT

Printed in Mexico

ISBN: 978-0-544-07214-5

9 10 0908 21 20 19 18 17

4500669231   A B C D E F G

➤ **Look for each word in yellow along with its meaning.**

sun	moon	magnify
star	phases	
shadow	telescope	

➤ **Underlined sentences answer these questions.**

What can we see in the daytime sky?

How does the daytime sky seem to change?

What can we see in the nighttime sky?

How does the nighttime sky seem to change?

How can we look at objects in the sky?

What can we see in the daytime sky?

It is day. <u>We can see the sun.</u> The sun is the closest star to Earth. A star is an object in the sky. A star gives off its own light.

Look out the window. Can you see the sun?

sky

sun

clouds

How does the daytime sky seem to change?

Clouds move and change in the sky.

The sun seems to move across the sky.

The sun does not move. Earth moves.

Earth turns every day. Earth goes around the sun, too.

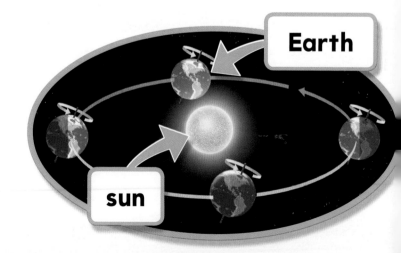

Earth

sun

The shadow of the ball changes during the day.

| morning | noon | afternoon |

A shadow is a dark spot made when an object blocks sunlight. Shadows change during the day. They change because Earth is moving. The sun's light shines on objects from different directions as the day goes on.

What can we see in the nighttime sky?

The sky gets dark at night. The place on Earth where you are standing is not facing the sun. You can usually see the moon. The moon is a large sphere of rock.

The moon does not give off its own light.

The sun is a star, too. You can not see it at night.

You can still see clouds at night.

You can also see stars in the nighttime sky. The stars look very tiny. They are very far away. Closer stars look bigger. Clouds sometimes cover the stars or moon.

How does the nighttime sky seem to change?

The moon's shape seems to change as it moves around Earth. The different shapes we see are called phases.

It takes about 29 days for the moon to go around Earth.

first quarter   full   third quarter

Earth goes around the sun. The seasons change. In each season, you see different stars. The stars you do not see are behind the sun.

The sky looks different in each season.

How can we look at objects in the sky?

You can use a telescope to look at the sky. A telescope is a tool to make things look big. A telescope will magnify what you are looking at. Magnify means to make something look bigger.

telescope

Telescope lenses make things look big.

Eyeglass lenses also make things look big.

This picture was taken through a telescope.

An eyeglass maker made the first telescope. Then a scientist made a telescope that uses mirrors. Telescopes today use lenses and mirrors.

What would you look at if you could use this telescope?

Use a Magnifier!

Use a hand lens to look at a word in this book. Then take the hand lens away and look at the word again. What does the hand lens do? Share your observations with a friend.

 ## Write About the Moon

Which phase of the moon do you like the best? Draw your favorite phase. Then tell a friend about your drawing.